Odes To My Lord

Odes To My Lord

Elba Soler

ODES TO MY LORD

NIV
Scripture quotations marked NIV are taken from the Holy Bible, New International Version®. NIV®. Copyright © 1973, 1978, 1984 by International Bible Society. Used by permission of Zondervan. All rights reserved. [Biblica]

iUniverse books may be ordered through booksellers or by contacting:

iUniverse
1663 Liberty Drive
Bloomington, IN 47403
www.iuniverse.com
1-800-Authors (1-800-288-4677)

ISBN: 978-1-5320-7921-4 (sc)
ISBN: 978-1-5320-7920-7 (hc)
ISBN: 978-1-5320-7922-1 (e)

Library of Congress Control Number: 2019910504

Print information available on the last page.

iUniverse rev. date: 07/26/2019

Contents

Introduction

This is a book of poetry that will reach your heart and move you to tears. Between rhyme and rhythm, feel the deepest sentiments found in love and rancor, anxiety and liberation... Written catharsis!

I Was Born!

I was born in the enchanted island of Puerto Rico, USA, to a military dad. My parents were divorced when I was nine. I was uprooted and tossed about between them and my grandmother. I went to nine different schools, which made it very difficult to "grow" relationships. During my growing years I felt like a flower that was cut and not allowed to bloom; dehydrated and uprooted, neglected and forgotten, deprived of care and affection...

Not having a stable home, I felt like I didn't belong anywhere... Until one day, I read John 14:1-6 and my eyes were opened... There <u>was</u> a place a place for me, and Jesus himself was preparing it for me! For the first time in my life I felt I belonged! I felt like I was just born!...

Well, not knowing how to express myself or who to turn to, I poured out my heart into my poetry. These poems are a reflection of how I felt. Read on and feel...

As You Cross The Bridge

As you cross the bridge

That transcends

From a single life

To another of commitment,

Remember the old proverb:

"It is better to give

Than to receive."

Give it all,

So joy can be achieved.

Soon you will take the step

That will tie your destiny

Of giving yourself

Fully to the one you love,

To fill the void

We all have.

"Two will come together

To become one,"

As it states in the Bible,

God said:

"It is not good

for man to be alone."

As two half-full cups,

It is necessary to pour one

Into the other,

So both will be fulfilled.

Life is full of hues;

Vivid colors, and gray ones too;

They compliment each other.

You will have highs,

And you will have lows.

But if both share the same feeling,

And only one thought:

To make the other happy;

When one is down,

You will extend out your hand

To bring up your partner;

And thus, when you see the other smile,

Joy will fill both your hearts!

Elba Soler

3/2/2010

Valdosta, GA

Before you I kneel

Dear Lord,

Before you I kneel;

I can't express what I feel,

But you keep me on an even keel.

You provide my everyday meal,

And before I even appeal,

I know my prayer you hear, (Matthew 21:22)

Because all your sheep bear your seal,

And all of them you steer,

And watch over them with zeal. (John 10:11)

Elba Soler

Valdosta, GA

3/28/2006

Be Stingy

Be stingy with your complaints,

But be generous with your compliments.

They say I'm so stingy,

I even use few words.

But I'd rather just listen,

Than impose my views on them.

If I can't say something positive,

I'd rather not make any comment.

I have found that when my mouth is open,

I can't hear what others have spoken.

Maybe that's today's problem;

People are too busy talking,

Sharing their opinions with "them",

Even if they don't edify,

But rather hurt, disparage and smother.

So I'll be stingy, for the moment,

With my complaints and comments,

So as not to hurt others.

Elba Soler

11/28/2017

Valdosta, GA

But Time

But is the bud

Of hopelessness.

But is getting stuck

In the mud;

You can spin your wheels around,

But only a positive wedge

Will get you out of the rut.

Negativity is a malignancy;

Stop it, or it will stop you.

Doubt is a cloud…

But there is no clout in doubt.

Failure to believe,

Breeds failure to try;

Failure to try is failure.

Attitude affects our actions;

Belief determines behavior;

Together they spell BIG things.

Active faith is alive.

Fail to act, and you die.

Therefore, redeem the time.

Everyone has been given time.

What counts

is what you do with it…

You will be called

To give account.

Time is no respecter of persons.

Eat healthy, exercise, stay fit…

But time will not stay still

The world turns, the clock turns,

And any way you turn,

When it's your turn,

Time will run out in the end.

Today is a gift;

That's why it's called: the present.

So don't waste it.

Wasting is a sin.

Call it whatever you want,

But sin is still sin.

Time is a relative means

By which we measure

The passing of events;

What we've done with it

Is our treasure!

Elba Soler

Valdosta, GA

2/1/2010

Leaves

Because I don't rake the leaves

They call me slovenly;

But I like to see the leaves;

They keep me company.

I watch them stir,

And move and tremble

As if tickled by the breeze;

And twirl and tumble,

Swinging in the wind,

Until they kiss the ground beneath

At the foot of the tree.

Elba R. Soler
Valdosta, GA 1/2/2015

©Many Colors - Song ♫

Many colors are the flowers

That abound all around;

Many colors are the flowers

That adorn our little house;

Many colors are the flowers

That bloom all the time;

Many colors are the flowers

That God our Father for us provides,

Many colors are the flowers

And I thank Him from my heart,

Many colors are the flowers
And my God is only one!

Elba Soler

7/23/2011

Valdosta, GA

Dear God: It's Me...

Dear God: It's me.

I know you're here;

I see you in the sunshine,

I feel you in the breeze

That gently stirs

The tree leaves.

In my hour of grief

I do not despair,

For you comfort me,

And all is fair.

In the grand scheme

Of things

I'm but a speck;

Yet I know all you've created

Has its own place.

Let me be the vessel

To carry your great Blessings;

Help me to follow

In your Son's footsteps;

As He himself said;

"I came here to serve,

Not to be served." (Mathew 20:28)

Elba Soler

Valdosta, GA

10/15/2012

Every Time The Fool

Every time the fool

Disregards instruction,

And chooses to disobey,

There will be a price to pay.

If the fool refuses to pray

And chooses

To go his own way,

The devil is no fool,

And not too far away,

And always ready to prey;

For it is written:

"Wide is the road

That leads to destruction,

And very narrow the one

That leads to salvation;

And very few the ones

Who find it!" (Mathew 7:13)

Elba Soler

Valdosta, GA

3/28/2006

GOD Reigns

How awesome

When you wonder

About unexplainable events;

Then you realize

God was behind them.

What some may call coincidence,

I call providence.

God is sovereign;

For nothing happens

In this world

Without His intervention.

Regardless of our intentions;

God reigns.

It maybe raining outside,

But God reigns in my heart.

It may be dark out,

But Light still shines inside...

God reigns.

Elba Soler

Valdosta, GA

1/20/2015

©How Marvelous It Is - Song ♫

How marvelous it is

When the sun shines;

How awesome when it hides

In the clouds;

But much more wonderful

And comforting

Is the love the SON sheds on me.

//How marvelous it is,

How wonderful it is,

The love my Lord gives to me. //

Elba Soler

12/5/2018 12pm

Valdosta, GA

©I Sinned - &ong ♫

I sinned; My God, forgive me.
I plead for mercy, please!

// Though I have sinned so greatly,
Your mercy's greater still… //

Through your blood, so precious,
I have been redeemed;

// Though I have sinned so gravely,
Your mercy's greater still… //

Elba Soler
2/3/2019
Valdosta, GA

I Weep Through My Pen

Youth, divine treasure,

Gone forever,

Never to return,

With the elusive dream

Of yesterday,

Washed away by the rain.

Deflowered

And withered rose

Of love,

All illusion

Killed by pain;

Sometimes

When I grief

The tears won't flow;

Other times,

I weep through my pen...

Elba Soler

8/3/2012

Valdosta, GA

I'm Not Alone

I went to the shore

By the sea

And the waves said to me

You no longer loved me;

Despondent,

I responded:

"I don't know

Why my love is so.

Is there no hope?"

Then I heard

A voice from above:

"There's no need

To weep;

My love for you is so deep,

Your tears I can't bear to see."

Then heaven was moved

To compassion

And tears from above

Came down and touched

My aching soul.

I felt the soft wind

Caressing my skin,

Playing with my hair,

And all my cares

Vanished into thin air.

I saw the Son show

His love

Through His warm glow.

I saw the Light

And my plight

Departed;

As the clouds parted,

It no longer mattered

That you were gone,

For now I know

I'm not alone!

Elba Soler

4/30/2009

Valdosta, GA

©If You Had Any Faith - &ong ♫

//If you had any faith

As little as a grain of mustard seed,

That is what the Lord says\\

You could say

Unto the mountain:

//Move away\\

You could say

Unto the mountain:

//Move away\\

And the mountain

Will ///move away\\\

And the mountain

Will ///move away\\\

//////Move away\\\\\\

And the mountain

Will move away!

Elba Soler

Valdosta, IL. 2006

©In The Morning When I Rise - Song ♫

In the morning when I rise,

I sing praises to my Lord.

When surrounded by my plight,

I seek Him for His Comfort.

When adversity I must confront,

I cry out to my only Lord.

And He that is true and faithful

Will be there as my protector.

\\In the troubling days to come

I know I won't be alone...//

There are those who love money,

But I only adore my Lord.

There are those that seek fame and glory,

But I follow the One I love.

There are those who have fear of nothing,

But I fear my God above.

And He that is true and faithful

Will be there as my protector.

\\In the troubling days to come

I know He will take me home...//

Elba Soler – Valdosta, GA 2008

Jesus Told This Story

Jesus told this story:
"I left my throne of glory;
For you, I was nailed to a tree;"
Said He, who gave his life for me.
"With my own life
I paid the price,
So you wouldn't suffer the strife
And fires of hell,
In spite of your sins;
Because my love is infinite
And I'm with you 'til the end.
I've come here,
down to Earth,
to love, comfort and heal.
Whatever you say
or think, I hear.

I know how you feel.

Remember, I know pain and grief,

And have shed many tears. (John 11:35)

So let me allay your fears;

Put your trust in me."

Elba Soler

Valdosta, GA

4/8/2009

©Let Us Give Thanks - Song ♫

//Let us give thanks to the Lord,

Let us thank Him,

Let us thank Him for His love.//

In the mornings

The birds all thank Him.

Singing their praises

To the triune God;

And you my friend,

Why don't you join 'em,

Singing your praises

To our loving God…

//Let us give thanks to the Lord,

Let us thank Him,

Let us thank Him for His love.//

Elba Soler

10/4/18

Valdosta, GA

Like The Dew

Like the dew

In the morning

Touches the grass

When it's wilting,

So is man

In his mourning;

God's loving spirit

Touches his heart

And even in his grief

He finds relief.

Elba Soler

Valdosta, GA

8/3/2012

My Husband

My Husband,

My lover,

My confidant,

My soul brother,

My companion,

My life-partner,

My best friend.

Elba R. Soler

5/6/2019

Gimpy, but not wimpy! (His own words)

*His favorite quotes from the JC Creed: *
THE JAYCEE CREED

We believe:

*That faith in God gives meaning and purpose to human life;

*That the brotherhood of man transcends the sovereignty of nations;

- That economic justice can best be won by free men through free enterprise;

- That government should be of laws rather than of men;

- *That earth's great treasure lies in human personality; and

  *That service to humanity is the best work of life.

Rejoice Through The Tears

Rejoice through the tears,

My dear,

For God is near.

Listen close,

As He whispers in your ear:

"Let your heart not be troubled...

I go to prepare

A place for you,

So where I am, there

You may also be." (John 14:1-3)

I love you so much,

For you

I was nailed to a tree.

You are not forsaken;

I have taken

Your loved one Home,

To wait there

For you

With Me.

Like a day flower,

Here today,

Gone tomorrow,

So is your sorrow

Here on earth.

So do not fret,

Today you may be mourning,

But God promises

Joy in the morning; (Ps. 30:5)

Tomorrow will give birth

To a new day...

And your troubles will seem

So far away!

Elba R. Soler
Valdosta, GA
8/20/2003

I wrote this to a friend's daughter, who had lost her mother to Cancer.

I would like this read at my funeral.

When I die, don't cry.

Don't be sad, but rather be glad.

Rejoice in the thought that

I'll be singing to my greatest love.

No more pain, no more sorrow,

No fear of tomorrow...

Snow White

When October comes around,

I like to see the snow-white covered ground;

Not the cold snow of the North,

Though awesome to look at

When I'm inside looking out,

But the cotton covered ground

Of the warm, beautiful South!

Elba Soler

10/22/2018

Valdosta, GA

I was so taken when I first saw a snow-white cotton field; it reminded me of when I first saw snow on the ground in Chicago. I was 4, coming out of Kinder Garden. Although I lived in Chicago most of my life, I'm in love with Georgia, and I met the love of my life here. I don't miss the snow, because a white cotton field looks like fresh fallen snow, but without the cold!

Thank you, God

Thank you, God,

For bringing me to Georgia;

I'm so blessed

To be here in Valdosta;

Even though it's foggy, muddy,

And pest infested...

But the people are so nice,

Hospitable and friendly,

That 'though kinship

I have here none,

I don't feel alone;

I feel right at home

Because of their friendship.

True, there are no jobs

Of any consequence,

Or monetary recompense.

Here, it's not what you know,

But who you know

That matters any.

You know I've spent

A pretty penny

In education

And license preparation…

All to no avail,

But I do not wail.

All my needs

You have provided;

My hunger you feed

with plenty of food;

Just look at my hips…

There is the proof!

Elba Soler
Valdosta, GA 7/19/2009

©There Is A Way - Song ♫

There is a way

The world does not know;

There is a way

I would like to show.

//In Christ you'll find

The Way, the Truth, the Life;

In Christ you'll find

The Way to eternal life.\\

There is a way

The world does not know;

There is a way

You can save your soul.

\\In Christ you'll find

The Way, the Truth, the Life;

In Christ you'll find

The Way to eternal life.//

Elba Soler

9/4/2018

Panama City, FL

©There is Fire - Song ♫

\\There is fire

Deep, deep within my heart//

Since the Lord, Jesus Christ,

Came into my heart

There is fire

And I can't put it out.

\\If you want

Some fire in your heart//

Then come to Jesus Christ

And He will light your fire,

\\For Jesus will keep it

Kindling in your heart.//

\\This world

Very soon shall pass//

But the fire of love

Will never be put out,

\\For Jesus will stoke

The fire in your heart.//

Elba Soler

Bensenville, IL-1991

Welcome

Welcome,

Whoever is knocking

At the door of my soul.

Welcome,

So you can see

That I am waiting

With all my love.

If you've left your old love,

I bless you.

It's not so hard to forgive

All your misdeeds;

Even if I have to end

Buried in a grave;

If you can no longer fend,

Come to me,

I will give you strength.

Trust me,

I am your friend...

Al the way to the end!

Elba Soler

Valdosta, GA

2/24/2018

What Should I Do?

What should I do?

Where can I go?

Can somebody tell me;

For I do not know?

Why must I live,

If nobody wants me,

If nobody loves

This wandering soul;

If I am to live

And die all alone?

Do you know the answer?

Then tell me, oh Lord!

I'm so desperate…

Have mercy; have mercy

On this poor soul!

Don't abandon me,

Now that life's so dull;

Now that all around me

Has no meaning at all;

Now that my love

Has left me,

Now that my love

Is gone…

What should I do?

Where can I go?

Tell me, oh Lord! Tell me!

For I do not know!

Elba Soler

7/8/1967 12:00

Río Piedras, P.R.

.

Printed in the United States
By Bookmasters